Girls' Night In

MARKS & SPENCER

Marks and Spencer p.l.c.
PO Box 3339,
Chester CH99 9QS

shop online
www.marksandspencer.com

ISBN: 978-1-84805-676-3

Printed in China

Edited by Julie Whitaker and Ian Whitelaw
Internal design by Fiona Roberts

Notes for the Reader
This book uses both metric and imperial measurements. Follow the same units of measurement throughout; do not mix metric and imperial. All spoon measurements are level; teaspoons are assumed to be 5 ml and tablespoons are assumed to be 15 ml. Unless otherwise stated, milk is assumed to be full fat, individual vegetables such as potatoes are medium, and pepper is freshly ground black pepper. Recipes using raw or very lightly cooked eggs should be avoided by infants, the elderly, pregnant women, convalescents and anyone suffering from an illness. Pregnant and breastfeeding women are also advised to avoid eating peanuts and peanut products. The times given are an approximate guide only. Preparation times differ according to the techniques used by different people and the cooking times may also vary from those given. Please consume alcohol responsibly. Participation in the games and activities described in this book, and the related consumption of alcoholic drinks, is entirely the responsibility of the individual, and neither the author, the publishers, nor their agents can accept liability for such participation or consumption, or the rules, procedure, or outcome of any game contained herein. All consumption of alcohol is entirely at the participant's own risk.

Contents

Time to
Stay In!

Today, **women** can have it all. Gone are the days of a girl's life being mapped out in nappies and housework. Now, more than ever, women from every walk of life are realizing that sometimes we all need to take a break from the world and invite the **girls** round for a good old giggle. Our friends are there through thick and thin, and if we haven't seen them in a while, what better reason to throw a **party**? Getting together with your closest **girly pals** is about female bonding, escape, relaxation, letting your hair down and catching up. Whether you're **celebrating** something particular or rallying round a certain friend in times of need, a night with the girls is always what the doctor ordered.

As many **lifestyle gurus** will tell you, 'staying in' is definitely the new 'going out'. Twenty-first century women have discovered that **entertaining** the girls at home is the ideal way to keep in regular touch with old and new friends alike. Balancing hectic careers, demanding partners and families can be tough, and for many of us spare time is often a luxury. But every girl agrees that putting aside quality time for our friends has become more important than ever. So, here's a crash course to ensure that every **Girls' Night In** is an instant hit.

Planning Your 'Girls Only' Shindig

✳ Setting a date is crucial. This means that you must set a date when everyone is free and stick to it – even if it is a few weeks away. This has the added bonus that you have time to plan and get excited!

✳ Create some girly space. If you live in a shared flat or house, make sure that your male housemates are out of the way. If you have a family, organize a babysitter and send your man out for the evening.

✳ Clear your diary the night before and the night after if possible. It's far nicer to enjoy the evening than to turn up exhausted and spend the evening looking forward to bedtime!

✳ If you're hosting the party, set aside some time to clean up a little so that you don't have to worry that if your guests use the bathroom they will see a pile of washing and a grubby bath!

✳ Make sure you're not interrupted. Tell work colleagues, sisters or mums that you won't be accepting any phone calls – or worse still, uninvited visitors!

So, now you've cleared your schedule and sent the men away; what sort of evening would you like? For a **'Perfect Party Night'**, this chapter has fab recipes for a casual, impromptu party, with the focus on lots of laughter and no fuss. Stick on your favourite party tunes, or dig out old photographs for a great girly giggle. Or, how about a **'Home Health Spa'**? Nourish the body as well as the soul with revitalizing and wonderfully tasty food and drinks. Find out how to detox at home while having fun with your pals! At the end of a long week there is nothing better than a **'Movies & Munchies Night'**. This wickedly tempting chapter offers you fantastic recipes for classic munchies. So, take the phone off the hook and snuggle up with the girls to enjoy classic chick flicks such as *Pretty Woman*, *Love Actually*, *Bridget Jones* and many more. Why not throw a *Sex And The City* party with a dress code that says feminine and fun? **'Elegant Suppers'** will provide guidance on everything you need, from posh nosh to classic cocktails – and even the perfect after-dinner speech. So dust off those strappy kitten heels and get dressed up for the girls!

Perfect Party Night

Fun, friends and fantastic food – whether it's an impromptu

gathering with your girlfriends or one that's been planned for ages,

party nights in can be as relaxed or as wild as you like.

With an array of delicious but simple recipes, classic cocktails

and a few amusing drinking games, you'll never

want to party anywhere else!

Salmon Fingers
with Potato Wedges

serves 2

140 g/5 oz fine polenta or cornmeal

1 tsp paprika

400 g/14 oz salmon fillet, skinned and
sliced into 12 chunky fingers

1 egg, beaten

sunflower oil, for frying

salt and pepper

for the potato wedges

500 g/1 lb 2 oz potatoes, scrubbed
and cut into thick wedges

1–2 tbsp olive oil

½ tsp paprika

salt

☀ Preheat the oven to 200°C/400°F/Gas Mark 6. To make the potato wedges, dry the wedges on a clean tea towel. Spoon the oil into a roasting tin and put into the preheated oven briefly to heat. Toss the potatoes in the warm oil until well coated. Sprinkle with paprika and salt to taste and roast for 30 minutes, turning halfway through, until crisp and golden.

☀ Meanwhile, mix the cornmeal and paprika together on a plate. Dip each salmon finger into the beaten egg, then roll in the cornmeal mixture until the fingers are evenly coated.

☀ Heat enough oil to cover the base of a large, heavy-based frying pan over a medium heat. Carefully arrange half the salmon fingers in the pan and cook for 6 minutes, turning halfway through, until golden. Drain on kitchen paper and keep warm while you cook the remaining fingers.

☀ Serve with the potato wedges.

Thai Tofu Cakes
with Chilli Dip

serves 2–3

300 g/10½ oz firm tofu, coarsely grated

1 lemon grass stalk, finely chopped

2 garlic cloves, chopped

2.5-cm/1-inch piece fresh root ginger, grated

2 shallots, finely chopped

2 fresh red chillies, deseeded and finely chopped

4 tbsp chopped fresh coriander

90 g/3¼ oz plain flour

½ tsp salt

sunflower oil, for frying

for the chilli dip

3 tbsp white distilled vinegar or rice wine vinegar

2 spring onions, finely sliced

1 tbsp caster sugar

2 fresh chillies, finely chopped

2 tbsp chopped fresh coriander

pinch of salt

To make the chilli dip, mix all the ingredients together in a small serving bowl and set aside.

Mix the tofu with the lemon grass (discard the outer layer), garlic, ginger, shallots, chillies and coriander in a mixing bowl. Stir in the flour and salt to make a coarse, sticky paste. Cover and chill in the refrigerator for 1 hour to allow the mixture to firm up slightly.

Form the mixture into large walnut-sized balls and, using floured hands, flatten into rounds until you have 8 cakes. Heat enough oil to cover the base of a large, heavy-based frying pan over a medium heat. Cook the cakes in 2 batches, turning halfway through, for 4–6 minutes, or until golden brown.

Drain on kitchen paper and serve warm with the chilli dip.

Grilled Tuna
and Vegetable Kebabs

serves 4

4 tuna steaks, about 140 g/5 oz each

2 red onions

12 cherry tomatoes

1 red pepper, deseeded and diced into 2.5-cm/1-inch pieces

1 yellow pepper, deseeded and diced into 2.5-cm/1-inch pieces

1 courgette, sliced

1 tbsp chopped fresh oregano

4 tbsp olive oil

pepper

lime wedges, to garnish

to serve

selection of salads, cooked couscous, new potatoes or bread

Preheat the grill to high. Cut the tuna into 2.5-cm/1-in pieces. Peel the onions, leaving the root intact, and cut each onion lengthways into 6 wedges.

Divide the fish and vegetables evenly between 8 wooden skewers (pre-soaked to avoid burning) and arrange on the grill pan.

Mix the oregano and oil together in a small bowl. Season to taste with pepper. Lightly brush the kebabs with the oil and cook under the preheated grill for 10–15 minutes or until evenly cooked, turning occasionally. If you cannot fit all the kebabs on the grill pan at once, cook them in batches, keeping the cooked kebabs warm while cooking the remainder. Alternatively, these kebabs can be cooked on a barbecue.

Garnish with lime wedges and serve with a selection of salads and cooked couscous, new potatoes or bread.

Spanish Spinach
and Tomato Mini-Pizzas

makes 32

2 tbsp Spanish olive oil, plus
extra for brushing and drizzling

1 onion, finely chopped

1 garlic clove, finely chopped

400 g/14 oz canned chopped
tomatoes

125 g/4½ oz baby spinach leaves

salt and pepper

25 g/1 oz pine kernels

bread dough

100 ml/3½ fl oz warm water

½ tsp easy-blend dried yeast

pinch of sugar

200 g/7 oz strong white
flour, plus extra for dusting

½ tsp salt

To make the dough, measure the water into a small bowl, sprinkle in the dried yeast and sugar and leave in a warm place for 10–15 minutes, or until frothy. Meanwhile, sift the flour and salt into a large bowl. Make a well in the centre of the flour, pour in the yeast liquid and mix together with a wooden spoon. Using your hands, work the mixture until it leaves the sides of the bowl clean. Then, knead the dough on a lightly floured work surface for 10 minutes, until smooth and elastic. Shape into a ball and put it in a clean bowl. Cover with a clean, damp tea towel and leave in a warm place for 1 hour, or until it has risen and doubled in size.

To make the topping, heat the olive oil in a large, heavy-based frying pan. Add the onion and fry for 5 minutes, or until softened but not browned. Add the garlic and fry for a further 30 seconds. Stir in the tomatoes and cook for 5 minutes, until reduced to a thick mixture. Add the spinach leaves and cook, stirring, until wilted a little. Season with salt and pepper.

Preheat the oven to 200°C/400°F/Gas Mark 6. Knead the dough well for another 2–3 minutes. Roll it out very thinly and cut out 32 rounds. Place on lightly oiled baking trays.

Spread each base with the spinach mixture and sprinkle with pine kernels. Drizzle a little olive oil over each pizza. Bake in the oven for 10–15 minutes, until golden brown. Serve hot.

Satay Sauce

makes about 225 ml/8 fl oz

4 spring onions, coarsely chopped

1 garlic clove, coarsely chopped

2 tsp chopped fresh root ginger

6 tbsp peanut butter

1 tsp muscovado sugar

1 tsp Thai fish sauce

2 tbsp soy sauce

1 tbsp chilli or Tabasco sauce

1 tsp lemon juice

salt

coarsely crushed peanuts, to garnish

☀ Put all the ingredients into the blender. Add 150 ml / 5 fl oz water and process to a purée.

☀ Transfer to a saucepan, season to taste with salt and heat gently, stirring occasionally. Transfer to a bowl and sprinkle with the crushed peanuts.

☀ Serve warm or cold. Delicious with chicken.

Cheese Straws

serves 4

vegetable oil or butter, for greasing

plain flour, for dusting

225 g/8 oz puff pastry,
thawed if frozen

2 tsp mustard (optional)

115 g/4 oz grated Cheddar cheese
or a mixture of Cheddar and
Parmesan cheese

cayenne pepper (optional)

 Preheat the oven to 200°C/400°F/Gas Mark 6. Grease a baking tray.

 Sprinkle the work surface with flour, then roll out the pastry to make a large rectangle.

 Spread the mustard, cheese and cayenne, if using, over the pastry, then cut it into thin strips about 10 cm/4 in long.

 Carefully arrange the straws on the baking tray, transfer to the oven and bake for 5–10 minutes, or until crisp and golden.

 Remove from the oven, leave to cool and then serve in baskets or piled high on plates.

Crispy Bacon Skewers

serves 4

12 streaky bacon rashers
12 stoned dates or prunes,
or raw scallops, shelled,
or water chestnuts

☀ Firmly holding down each bacon rasher in turn with a knife or fork on a chopping board, use a sharp knife to smooth and stretch the length.

☀ Place a date at one end of each rasher and roll up. Alternatively, you can use prunes, raw scallops or water chestnuts. Secure the roll with a cocktail stick to keep it closed.

☀ Preheat a ridged griddle or grill until very hot. Place the bacon rolls on the griddle or on the grill rack and cook, turning once, for 5–10 minutes, or until the bacon is crisp and well browned. Whatever is wrapped in the bacon must be thoroughly cooked or heated through. Alternatively, you could cook the bacon rolls on a baking sheet for 25–30 minutes in an oven preheated to 200°C/400°F/Gas Mark 6.

☀ Transfer to a large platter and serve immediately.

Aïoli

serves 2

3 large garlic cloves,
finely chopped
2 egg yolks
225 ml/8 fl oz extra virgin olive oil
1 tbsp lemon juice
1 tbsp lime juice
1 tbsp Dijon mustard
1 tbsp chopped fresh tarragon
salt and pepper
1 fresh tarragon sprig, to garnish

☀ Ensure that all the ingredients are at room temperature. Place the garlic and egg yolks in a food processor and process until well blended. With the motor running, pour in the oil, teaspoon by teaspoon, through the feeder tube until the mixture starts to thicken, then pour in the remaining oil in a thin stream until a thick mayonnaise forms.

☀ Add the lemon and lime juices, mustard and tarragon, and season to taste with salt and pepper. Blend until smooth, then transfer to a non-metallic bowl. Garnish with a tarragon sprig.

☀ Cover with clingfilm and refrigerate until required.

Fried Potatoes
with Piquant Paprika

serves 6

3 tsp paprika

1 tsp ground cumin

¼–½ tsp cayenne pepper

½ tsp salt

450 g/1 lb small old
potatoes, peeled

sunflower oil, for shallow-frying

sprigs of fresh flat-leaved
parsley, to garnish

aïoli (see page 17), to serve (optional)

Put the paprika, cumin, cayenne pepper and salt in a small bowl and mix well together. Set aside.

Cut each potato into 8 thick wedges. Pour enough sunflower oil into a large, heavy-based frying pan so that it comes about 2.5 cm/1 in up the sides of the pan. Heat the oil, then add the potato wedges, preferably in a single layer, and fry gently for 10 minutes, or until golden brown all over, turning from time to time. Remove from the pan with a slotted spoon and drain on kitchen paper.

Transfer the potato wedges to a large bowl and, while they are still hot, sprinkle with the paprika mixture, then gently toss them together to coat.

Turn the fried potatoes with paprika into one large, warmed serving dish, several smaller ones or individual plates and serve hot, garnished with parsley sprigs. Accompany with a bowl of aïoli for dipping, if wished.

Fruit Skewers

serves 4

6 tbsp brown sugar

pinch of ground mixed spice

8 whole strawberries, hulled

3 nectarines, stoned and cut into
bite-sized chunks

400 g/14 oz canned pineapple chunks, drained

4 plums, stoned and cut into bite-sized chunks

6 tbsp butter, melted

chocolate almond sauce

125 g/4½ oz plain chocolate,
broken into small pieces

2½ tbsp butter

6 tbsp water

1 tbsp almond liqueur, such as Amaretto

chopped mixed nuts, to decorate

☀ Combine the sugar and mixed spice and spread out on a large plate.

☀ Thread the whole strawberries onto metal skewers, alternating with the chunks of nectarine, pineapple and plum. When the skewers are full (leave a small space at either end), brush them with melted butter, then turn them in the spiced sugar until lightly coated. Transfer to a barbecue or preheated grill pan and cook, turning occasionally, for 8–10 minutes.

☀ To make the sauce, gently melt the chocolate and butter with the water in a small saucepan, stirring constantly, until smooth. Stir in the almond liqueur.

☀ Remove the skewers from the heat. Divide between individual plates, decorate with chopped mixed nuts and serve hot with the chocolate almond sauce.

Chocolate Fondue

serves 4

4 tbsp caster sugar

4 tbsp water

250 g/9 oz plain chocolate, broken into small pieces

225 ml/8 fl oz double cream

2½ tbsp rum

to serve

cake cut into bite-sized pieces

small whole strawberries, hulled

cherries, stoned

kiwi fruit or pineapple, cut into bite-sized pieces

 Heat the sugar and water in a small saucepan over a low heat, stirring, until the sugar has dissolved. Remove from the heat and leave to cool a little.

 Heat the chocolate and cream in a separate small saucepan over a low heat, stirring, until the chocolate has melted. Remove the pan from the heat and stir in the rum. Stir the chocolate mixture into the sugar syrup.

 To serve, reheat the mixture in a fondue pot. Alternatively, reheat in a saucepan, then transfer to a flameproof dish and keep warm, over a small burner if you have one. Serve with pieces of cake and a selection of fruit for your guests to spear on fondue or table forks and dip into the warm mixture.

Tequila Slammer

serves 1

1 measure white tequila, chilled

1 measure lemon juice

sparkling wine, chilled

Slammers are also known as shooters. The idea is that you pour the ingredients directly into the glass, without stirring. Cover the glass with one hand to prevent spillage, slam it on to a table to mix and drink the cocktail down in one! Be sure to use a strong glass!

Put the tequila and lemon juice into a chilled glass.

Top up with sparkling wine.

Cover the glass with your hand and slam.

Sangria

serves 4–6

1 bottle full-bodied red wine

3 tbsp Cointreau

3 tbsp brandy

juice of 1 orange and 1 lime

1 tbsp caster sugar, or to taste

1 orange

1 lime

1 peach or red-skinned eating apple

to serve

300 ml/10 fl oz soda water
or lemonade

2 handfuls of ice cubes

✴ Pour the wine into a large jug or punch bowl. Add the Cointreau, brandy and orange and lime juices, then stir in the sugar.

✴ Cover and leave to chill in the refrigerator for 2 hours.

✴ When ready to serve, cut the orange and lime into thin slices. Cut the peach in half, remove and discard the stone and slice the flesh. Alternatively, cut the apple in half, remove and discard the core and thinly slice. Remove the sangria from the refrigerator and stir in the sliced fruit.

✴ To serve, add the soda water and ice cubes, stir well, then pour or ladle into wine glasses.

The Perfect
Cosmopolitan

serves 1

4–6 cracked ice cubes

2 measures vodka

½ measure Cointreau

1 measure cranberry juice

juice of ½ lime

to decorate

twist of lime rind

twist of lemon rind

☀ Put the cracked ice cubes into a cocktail shaker.

☀ Pour the vodka, Cointreau and cranberry juice over the ice. Add the lime juice and shake well, then strain into a cocktail glass.

☀ Decorate with a twist of lime rind and a twist of lemon rind.

Shirley Temple

serves 1

8–10 cracked ice cubes

2 measures lemon juice

½ measure grenadine

½ measure sugar syrup

ginger ale, to top up

to decorate

slice of orange

cocktail cherry

◉ Put 4–6 of the cracked ice cubes into a cocktail shaker.

◉ Pour the lemon juice, grenadine and sugar syrup over the ice and shake vigorously.

◉ Half fill a small, chilled glass with the remaining ice cubes and strain the cocktail over them. Top up with ginger ale.

◉ Decorate with a slice of orange and a cocktail cherry.

Fun Drinking Games

Drinking Straw Races

Number of players: 2–10

You will need: One or more empty ice-cube trays and a quantity of straws.

How to play:

❋ Although this game can be played by just two people, it is much more fun with a larger group, divided into teams.

❋ For two contestants only, fill two rows of an empty ice-cube tray with beer or some other alcoholic drink of your choice. Each player, armed with a straw and operating from opposite ends of the tray, endeavours to suck up all the alcohol in their row. The first to completely drain their row is the winner.

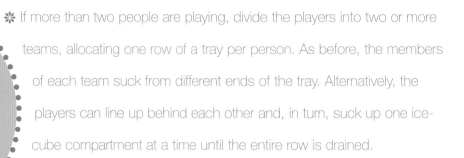

❋ If more than two people are playing, divide the players into two or more teams, allocating one row of a tray per person. As before, the members of each team suck from different ends of the tray. Alternatively, the players can line up behind each other and, in turn, suck up one ice-cube compartment at a time until the entire row is drained.

Spin the Bottle

Number of players: 4–10

You will need: An empty wine or beer bottle, lying on its side.

How to play:

Drinking games don't come much simpler than this.

❉ Everyone sits in a circle around a table or on the floor. Someone then spins the bottle firmly. Whoever the neck of the bottle is pointing to when it comes to a stop has to take a drink.

❉ A more elaborate variation of this game is to use a revolving circular cheeseboard, or some other flat object that can be spun. Stick small labels around the edge of the cheeseboard, representing different types of drinks – e.g. whisky, vodka, gin, wine, beer, fruit juice etc. You spin the cheeseboard and when it stops each player is given a drink of whatever is indicated on the sticker facing them. Make sure that you only label drinks that you have available.

Home Health Spa

Shut the world out, leave the phone off the hook and take

relaxation to the next level with your very own Home Health Spa.

With healthy and delicious recipes to detox and revitalize and a selection

of nourishing smoothies and juices, you can really let go. Why

not try a make-your-own face pack to ensure you look as

good on the outside as you feel on the inside?

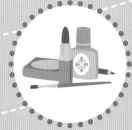

Lentil and
Goat's Cheese Salad

serves 4

115 g/4 oz dried Puy lentils

1 bay leaf

8 spring onions, finely chopped

225 g/8 oz red pepper, diced

1 tbsp chopped fresh parsley

450 g/1 lb cherry tomatoes,
sliced in half

for the dressing

4 tsp olive oil

4 tsp balsamic vinegar

2 tsp runny honey

4 cloves garlic, peeled and
crushed or finely chopped

225 g/8 oz rocket

140 g/5 oz goat's cheese,
sliced or crumbled

 Rinse the lentils and put in a medium-sized saucepan. Add the bay leaf and cover with plenty of cold water, bring to the boil then reduce the heat and simmer for 20–30 minutes or until the lentils are tender.

 Drain the lentils and transfer to a bowl. Add the spring onions, red pepper, parsley and cherry tomatoes. Mix well.

 Whisk together the oil, vinegar, honey and garlic and stir into the lentils. Serve on a bed of rocket, with the goat's cheese sprinkled over.

Cook's Tip

If time is short, replace the dried lentils with 350 g/12 oz (drained weight) canned cooked lentils.

Chilli Beef and Black-eyed Beans

serves 4

4 tsp olive oil

2 large onions, finely chopped

4 cloves garlic, crushed or finely chopped

3 green peppers

350 g/12 oz extra lean braising steak

4 tsp concentrated vegetable stock

2 tbsp tomato purée

2 green chillies, finely chopped

200 g/7 oz canned black-eyed beans

200 g/7 oz canned tomatoes, chopped

2 tsp chilli sauce

pepper

225 g/8 oz white rice

2 tbsp chopped fresh coriander,
to garnish (optional)

✷ Heat the oil in the non-stick frying pan and sauté the onion, garlic and green peppers (chop peppers into 1-cm/½-in squares before adding) over a medium heat for 2–3 minutes until the onion is soft and just turning golden.

✷ Cut the beef into very small pieces and add to the pan. Cook until browned all over. Add the stock, tomato purée, chillies, beans, tomatoes and chilli sauce, and season to taste. Stir well, bring to a simmer, cover and reduce the heat.

✷ Cook for 30 minutes, then check the dish for heat, seasoning and dryness. Add extra chilli sauce or very finely chopped fresh chillies (make sure they are deseeded). Add water if the sauce looks too dry.

✷ Cook for a further 25–30 minutes until the meat is tender. Meanwhile, cook the rice according to packet instructions. Drain and transfer the cooked rice to a warm plate, spoon over the sauce and garnish with coriander, if desired.

Chicken, Mushroom and Butternut Squash

serves 2

for the stuffing

7 g/¼ oz dried mushrooms

100 ml/3½ fl oz boiling water

1 tsp olive oil

50 g/1¾ oz fresh brown-cap mushrooms, finely chopped

25 g/1 oz 95 per cent fat-free soft cheese

2 x 125 g/4½ oz skinless chicken breasts

2 slices Parma ham, trimmed of any fat

for the squash

625 g/1lb 6oz butternut squash, deseeded and cut into 2-cm/¾-in chunks

2 tbsp chopped fresh rosemary

2 tbsp chopped fresh oregano

pepper

1 tsp olive oil

☀ Preheat the oven to 180°C/350°F/Gas Mark 4.

☀ Pour boiling water over the dried mushrooms. Leave to stand for 5 minutes. Drain and finely chop. Heat the oil in a non-stick saucepan, add the fresh and dried mushrooms and cook for about 10 minutes or until they are beginning to brown and any liquid has evaporated. Cool. Put the soft cheese in a bowl, stir in the mushrooms and season to taste.

☀ Using a sharp knife, make a slit lengthways in each chicken breast to form a pocket. Spoon in the mushroom mixture. Wrap one slice of ham around each breast and enclose in foil to make a parcel.

☀ Put the chunks of squash into a roasting tin. Add the herbs and pepper, drizzle with oil and stir to coat. Place the chicken parcels on top of the squash and bake for 30 minutes. Remove the foil and return the chicken and squash to the oven for 10 minutes, or until the chicken is cooked. Serve immediately.

Tofu and Vegetable Stir-fry and Rice Noodles

serves 2

225 g/8 oz firm tofu, sliced into strips

2 tsp vegetable oil

100 g/3½ oz pak choi, roughly chopped

100 g/3½ oz broccoli florets, roughly chopped

2 small carrots, peeled and cut into thin strips

50 g/1¾ oz beansprouts

2 tsp Thai green curry paste

4 tbsp vegetable stock

4 spring onions, trimmed and halved lengthways

100g/3½ oz rice noodles, to serve

for the marinade

2 tsp soy sauce

2 tbsp lime juice

2 tsp chopped garlic

2 tsp chopped lemon grass

2 tsp chopped root ginger

2 tsp chopped red chilli

 Drain the tofu, wash under cold running water and remove excess water with kitchen paper. Put the tofu in a shallow dish. To make the marinade, whisk together the soy sauce and lime juice and pour over the tofu with the other marinade ingredients. If possible, leave to marinate for at least 2 hours.

Cook the noodles according to packet instructions. Drain and keep warm.

Heat the oil in a non-stick wok or large frying pan. Remove the tofu from the marinade, reserving the marinade, and stir-fry the tofu for 1 minute. Add the pak choi, broccoli, carrots and beansprouts and cook, stirring, for a further minute.

In a small bowl or cup mix the curry paste, stock and reserved marinade. Add half to the stir-fry mixture and cook for another 2 minutes. Add the remaining paste to the marinade mix and the spring onions to the stir-fry and cook for a minute, or until the vegetables are just tender. Serve on a bed of warm noodles.

Warm Bean Salad

serves 6

1 tsp olive oil

1 red onion, peeled and finely chopped

2–3 garlic cloves, peeled and chopped

1 red chilli, deseeded and chopped

1 red pepper, deseeded and skinned

1 orange pepper, deseeded and skinned

300 g/10½ oz canned red kidney beans, drained and thoroughly rinsed

300 g/10½ oz can black-eyed beans, drained and thoroughly rinsed

300 g/10½ oz can flageolet beans, drained and thoroughly rinsed

200 ml/7 fl oz passata or tomato juice

1 tbsp sweet chilli sauce

100 g/3½ oz cherry tomatoes, halved

1 tbsp freshly chopped coriander

salt and pepper

warm strips of pitta bread, to serve

✸ Heat the oil in a large saucepan and gently sauté the onion, garlic and chilli for 3 minutes, stirring frequently. Cut the red and orange peppers into thin strips and thoroughly drain the beans.

✸ Add the peppers and beans to the saucepan together with the passata and sweet chilli sauce and season to taste. Bring to the boil, reduce the heat and cook for 10 minutes, or until the beans are piping hot. Add the halved tomatoes and heat gently for 2 minutes. Spoon into a serving bowl and sprinkle with the chopped coriander. Serve warm with strips of pitta bread.

Cook's Tip

If preferred, pass half the bean mixture through a food processor to form a chunky purée (you may need a little extra passata when blending). Return to the saucepan with the remaining whole beans and heat through gently.

Cod Loin
with Herb Crust

serves 4

4 pieces cod loin, about
115 g/4 oz each
4 garlic cloves
1 tbsp finely grated orange rind
2 tbsp chopped fresh parsley
2 tbsp chopped fresh dill
2 tbsp chopped fresh tarragon
pepper
4 tbsp orange juice
4 large tomatoes

to serve

butter bean purée
freshly cooked French beans

☀ Preheat the oven to 200°C/400°F/Gas Mark 6.

☀ Lightly rinse the fish and pat dry with kitchen paper. Crush 2 of the garlic cloves and mix with the orange rind, the herbs and a little pepper, then press one-quarter of the herb mixture onto each piece of fish. Place the pieces of fish in an ovenproof dish and pour the orange juice round them.

☀ Rinse and dry the tomatoes and cut in half. Cut the remaining garlic cloves into thin slivers and insert 3–4 slivers into each tomato half. Place on a dish and set aside.

☀ Place the fish in the oven and cook for 10 minutes, then add the tomatoes and cook with the fish for an additional 10 minutes, or until the fish is cooked.

☀ Serve with butter bean purée, the roasted tomatoes and French beans.

Cook's Tip

Take care not to overcook the fish, or it will be dry.

37

Rise and Shine Juice

serves 1

4 tomatoes, quartered

85 g/3 oz grated carrot

1 tbsp lime juice

☀ Put the tomatoes, carrot and lime juice into a blender and process for a few seconds until smooth.

☀ Place a nylon sieve over a bowl and pour in the tomato mixture. Using a spoon, gently push as much of the liquid through the sieve as possible. Discard any pips and pulp remaining in the sieve.

☀ Pour the juice into a glass and serve immediately.

Banana and Strawberry
Smoothie

☀ Put the banana, strawberries and yogurt into a blender and process for a few seconds until smooth.

☀ Pour into a glass and serve immediately.

serves 1

1 banana, sliced

100 g/3½ oz fresh strawberries, hulled

175 g/6 oz low-fat natural yogurt

Pear and
Chocolate Cream

serves 2

140 g/5 oz canned pears in juice
(drained weight)

140 g/5 oz virtually fat-free
fromage frais

few drops of vanilla essence

25 g/1 oz milk chocolate, grated

 Purée the pears in an electric blender, or mash thoroughly with a fork.

 In a mixing bowl, combine the pears, fromage frais and vanilla essence, then lightly stir in two-thirds of the chocolate.

 Spoon into two dessert glasses or dishes and top with the remaining chocolate. Chill before serving.

Detox Juice

This delicious energizer contains beetroot, one of the most effective liver-cleansing vegetables.

☀ Quarter the apples, then put them through a juicer along with the grapes, carrot, beetroot and ginger.

☀ Serve immediately.

serves 1

2 dessert apples

115 g/4 oz white seedless grapes

1 large carrot

55 g/2 oz cooked beetroot in natural juices

1-cm/½-inch piece of fresh root ginger

Melon and Ginger Sorbet

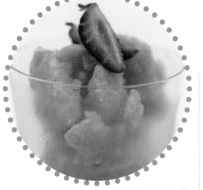

serves 4

1 ripe melon, peeled, deseeded
and cut into chunks
juice of 2 limes
1 tbsp grated fresh root ginger
4 tbsp unrefined caster sugar
1 egg white, lightly whisked
fresh strawberries or
raspberries, to serve

☀ Put the melon, lime juice and ginger into a food processor or blender and process until smooth. Pour into a measuring jug and make up to 600 ml/1 pint with cold water.

☀ Pour into a bowl and stir in the sugar. Beat in the egg white.

☀ Transfer to a freezerproof container and freeze for 6 hours.

☀ Serve in scoops with strawberries or raspberries.

Basic Body Detox

A daily and weekly body care routine, which you can easily carry out at home, will help improve the appearance of your skin and increase the elimination of toxins. It will also enhance your vitality and may help relieve digestive complaints. For extra pampering, treat yourself to at least one professional body treatment while detoxing.

Skin brushing

You lose about 0.5 kg/1 lb of waste products through the pores each day, so it makes sense to look after your skin. Brushing helps your skin 'breathe' efficiently by clearing the pores, and improves its appearance. It also boosts blood and lymph circulation, leading to more

efficient excretion of waste materials in the cells and helping to relieve water retention.

How to brush your skin

Use a long-handled, natural bristle brush, or a loofah or a dry flannel. Do not wet or moisturize your skin and avoid brushing the face – the skin here is very delicate. Strokes should be long and firm, and towards your heart. Spend about 5 minutes a day dry-brushing your skin, following the sequence below. Your skin will tingle and you should feel quite warm afterwards because you have stimulated your circulation.

❄ Start at your feet and work up your body. Brush both sides of your feet and up your legs.

❄ Brush towards the heart and over the breasts. Brush the stomach in gentle, circular strokes in a clockwise direction to follow the flow of your intestine.

❋ Raise each arm in turn and brush from the hand to the armpit.

❋ Brush from the buttocks up the back to the neck.

Daily shower or bath

Water can alter the body's blood flow and this can be manipulated by changing the water temperature. Hot water is relaxing. It dilates blood vessels, reducing blood pressure and increasing blood flow to the skin and muscles. The improved circulation helps remove waste products from the body and sends more oxygen and nutrients to the tissues to repair damage. Cold water is stimulating. It makes surface blood vessels constrict, restricting blood flow and sending blood towards the internal organs, helping them to function more efficiently. Having a warm bath or shower followed by a blast of cold water will do wonders for your circulation and skin.

Exfoliation

Exfoliation gently removes dead skin cells and should be done at least once a week. You can use the exfoliating body scrub or fill an old sock with oatmeal and swish it in your bath water. Once the oatmeal has softened, scrub your body with it. For a very gentle skin exfoliant, add 125 ml/4 fl oz apple cider vinegar to a lukewarm bath.

Exfoliating body scrub

You can buy a ready-made scrub or make your own at home (see recipe overleaf). The salt acts as an exfoliant, the oil or yogurt and honey moisturize the skin and the essential oil helps to clear the body of toxins.

Mix all the ingredients together in a bowl to make a runny paste.

1 tbsp sea salt

2 tbsp oil (olive, sunflower etc.) or yogurt

1 tbsp thick honey

2–3 drops of sweet marjoram, rose, sweet fennel or juniper oil

Exfoliating face scrub

Mix 1 tbsp of honey with 2 tbsp finely ground almonds and ½ tsp lemon juice. Rub gently on to face and rinse off with warm water.

How to exfoliate

❈ Relax in a warm bath for at least 10 minutes.

❈ Lift each limb out of the water and rub your exfoliating scrub in firm circles all over your body, paying particular attention to areas of hard skin (e.g. the heels). Kneel up and exfoliate your buttocks and back.

❈ Get out of the bath, gently pat yourself dry with a clean towel and apply a thick moisturizer or body oil.

Antioxidant face masks

❈ DRY SKIN: Take 1 tbsp of porridge oats and rub well between your fingers. Steep in a cup of boiling water for 20 minutes. Strain, then mix the oats with 1 tbsp honey, 1 egg yolk and 1 tbsp natural yogurt. Apply to the skin with cotton wool and leave on for 15 minutes.

❈ SENSITIVE SKIN: Mix 1 tsp aloe vera gel (available from pharmacies or healthfood stores) with 1 tbsp natural yogurt. Apply and leave for 15 minutes.

❈ OILY SKIN: Mix 1 tbsp dry fuller's earth (available from healthfood stores or pharmacies) with 1 egg yolk,

★ Use spa treatments on the day of making. Avoid contact with eyes. If treatment gets into the eyes, rinse well with warm water.

¼ mashed avocado and a little witch hazel to create a smooth mixture. Apply to the skin and leave on for 15 minutes.

✻ MATURE SKIN: Mash a ripe avocado with a little olive oil and apply to the skin. Leave on for 15 minutes.

Oils and emollients

After bathing or showering, you should always use oil or a good moisturizer to help your skin retain moisture. Essential oils help your skin to eliminate impurities as well as keeping it soft. Always use essential oils in a suitable carrier oil. Rub olive oil into patches of eczema, dandruff and psoriasis, both to reduce itching and promote healing.

Oils for face steaming

✻ DRY SKIN: Atlas cedarwood, geranium, neroli, rose, sandalwood.

✻ SENSITIVE SKIN: Jasmine, lavender, Roman chamomile, rosewood.

✻ OILY SKIN: Grapefruit, lemon grass, patchouli, sweet basil.

✻ MATURE SKIN AND WRINKLES: Clary sage, geranium, jasmine, lavender, rose, ylang-ylang.

Epsom salts baths

As part of your body detox regime, try having an Epsom salts bath every 5 days. Epsom salts are pure magnesium, which the body needs to help maintain healthy tissues, and it draws off toxins and improves circulation. Pour about 1 kg/2.2 lb. Epsom salts into bath water and stir until dissolved. Relax in the bath for 5 minutes, then massage your skin with a massage mitt or flannel.

★ *Use spa treatments on the day of making. Avoid contact with eyes. If treatment gets into the eyes, rinse well with warm water.*

Deep-clean your face once a week to remove impurities from skin pores. Start by cleaning your face using your normal cleanser. Next, fill a bowl with very hot water and add a few drops of an essential oil appropriate to your skin type. Lean over the bowl, with your head covered by a towel and your eyes closed, for 10 minutes. Use cotton wool to wipe your face clean, then soak your face using a warm, moist cloth. Apply a commercial skin mask suitable for your skin type, or make your own from the recipes provided. Leave it on for 15 minutes. Gently remove the face mask using a cool, wet cloth. Finally, apply a moisturizer.

you can. Massage essential oils into your hair to regulate hair-oil production and improve the condition of your scalp. Use 1 tbsp of carrier oil and 2 drops of essential oil. For greasy hair, choose from clary sage, geranium, lemon, lavender, tea tree, cypress and rosemary; for dry hair, choose from Roman chamomile (blond hair only), lavender and rosemary; and for dandruff, choose from tea tree, juniper, lemon, lavender and sandalwood.

Massage the oil into the scalp using your fingertips, leave for half an hour then rinse off. Towel hair dry and follow with the antioxidant fruit smoothie hair mask.

Scalp massage

A scalp massage and hair mask can help ensure glossy, healthy hair. Do this at least once a week if

Fruit smoothie hair mask

In a food processor or blender, mix ½ banana, ¼ melon, ¼ avocado, 1 tbsp olive oil and 1 tbsp yogurt. Work the mixture into the roots of your hair, then coat all the remaining hair. Wrap your head in clingfilm and leave for

★ Use spa treatments on the day of making. Avoid contact with eyes. If treatment gets into the eyes, rinse well with warm water.

15 minutes. Rinse your hair well in warm water then lightly shampoo and rinse again. Leave to dry naturally.

Hand massage

Gently stroke the front and back of each hand to relax and warm it. Mix 1 tbsp sea salt with 2 tsp olive oil and 3–4 drops lavender essential oil. Scoop the mixture into your hands and rub them together. Cover the entire hand and wrist area and leave for 1 minute. Rinse in warm water. Use your thumb to stroke from the knuckle of your little finger down the tendon towards the wrist. Repeat for each finger. Gently grip a finger with the knuckles of the first two fingers of the other hand. Slide down the finger to the fingertip, pulling with a corkscrew motion. Repeat twice on each finger and thumb. Use the opposite thumb to massage across the palm several times. Apply knuckle pressure to the palm

and then gently stroke it. Repeat the whole sequence on the other hand.

Foot massage

Fill a bowl with warm water and soak your feet for 10 minutes. Using a pumice stone, remove dead skin on the heels and sides of your feet. Apply some massage oil to your hands and rub firmly all over your foot and up over your ankle. Using your thumbs, massage the surface of your foot in tiny, deep circles. Do the same on the underside of your foot. Then massage up the inside edge of your foot, from the heel to the tip of the big toe. Wiggle your toes, then pull on each toe from the tip. Repeat the sequence for the other foot.

★ Use spa treatments on the day of making. Avoid contact with eyes. If treatment gets into the eyes, rinse well with warm water.

Movies & Munchies Night

What naughtiness! A well deserved night in with the girls,

complete with deliciously wicked treats such as home-made pizza

or a Marshmallow Float. The sofa is beckoning, so round up your

friends and choose from a selection of all-time classic movies.

Whether you want a good cry or a good laugh, there is a

movie listed in these pages for you.

Miniature
Pizzas

serves 4

115 g/4 oz strong white flour,
plus extra for dusting
½ tsp easy-blend dried yeast
½ tsp salt
1 tbsp olive oil
115–225 ml/4–8 fl oz warm water

topping

1 courgette
100 g/3½ oz passata
75 g/2¾ oz diced pancetta
50 g/1¾ oz black olives, stoned
and chopped
½ tbsp mixed dried herbs
1 tablespoon olive oil

☀ Mix the flour, yeast and salt together in a bowl. Drizzle over half the oil. Make a well in the flour and pour in the water. Mix to a firm ball of dough. Turn out onto a floured work surface and knead until it is no longer sticky. Add more flour if necessary. Grease the bowl with the remaining oil. Return the dough to the bowl and turn once to coat. Cover with a clean tea towel and leave to rise for 1 hour. When the dough has doubled in size, turn out and knock back to release excess air, then knead until smooth.

☀ To make the topping, grate the courgette finely. Cover with kitchen paper and leave to stand for 10 minutes to absorb some of the juices.

☀ Divide the dough into quarters and roll out into thin rounds. Place the dough rounds on a baking sheet, spread 2–3 tablespoons of the passata over the pizza bases and top each with the grated courgette, pancetta and olives. Season with pepper to taste and a sprinkling of mixed dried herbs and drizzle with olive oil.

☀ Bake in a preheated oven at 200°C/400°F/Gas Mark 6 for 15 minutes or until crispy. Season with salt and pepper to taste and serve hot.

The Ultimate Vegetarian Burger

serves 4–6

85 g/3 oz brown rice

400 g/14 oz canned flageolet beans, drained

115 g/4 oz unsalted cashew nuts

3 garlic cloves

1 red onion, cut into wedges

115 g/4 oz sweetcorn kernels

2 tbsp tomato purée

1 tbsp chopped fresh oregano

salt and pepper

2 tbsp wholemeal flour

2 tbsp sunflower oil

wholemeal buns

to garnish

green salad and slices of tomato

◉ Cook the rice in a saucepan of lightly salted boiling water for 20 minutes, or until tender. Drain and place in a food processor.

◉ Add the beans, cashew nuts, garlic, onion, sweetcorn, tomato purée, oregano and salt and pepper to the rice in the food processor and, using the pulse button, blend together. Shape into 4–6 equal-sized burgers, then coat in the flour. Cover and leave to chill for 1 hour.

◉ Heat a heavy-based frying pan and add the oil. When hot, add the burgers and cook over a medium heat for 5–6 minutes on each side or until cooked through and piping hot. Serve in wholemeal buns and add a green salad garnish with sliced tomatoes.

The Classic
Hamburger

serves 4–6

450 g/1 lb rump steak or
topside, freshly minced
1 onion, grated
2–4 garlic cloves, crushed
2 tsp wholegrain mustard
pepper
2 tbsp olive oil
450 g/1 lb onions, finely sliced
2 tsp light muscovado sugar
sesame seed buns

☀ Place the minced steak, onion, garlic, mustard and pepper in a large bowl and mix together. Shape into 4–6 equal-sized burgers, then cover and leave to chill for 30 minutes.

☀ Meanwhile, heat the oil in a heavy-based frying pan. Add the onions and sauté over a low heat for 10–15 minutes, or until the onions have caramelized. Add the sugar after 8 minutes and stir occasionally during cooking. Drain well on kitchen paper and keep warm.

☀ Wipe the frying pan clean, then heat until hot. When hot, add the burgers and cook for 3–5 minutes on each side or until cooked to personal preference. Serve in toasted sesame seed buns with the fried onions.

Nachos

serves 6

175 g/6 oz tortilla chips
400 g/14 oz canned refried
beans, warmed
2 tbsp finely chopped bottled
jalapeño chillies
200 g/7 oz canned or bottled
pimentos or roasted peppers,
drained and finely sliced
salt and pepper
115 g/4 oz Gruyère cheese, grated
115 g/4 oz Cheddar cheese, grated

☀ Preheat the oven to 200°C/400°F/Gas Mark 6.

☀ Spread the tortilla chips out over the base of a large, shallow, ovenproof dish
or roasting tin. Cover with the warmed refried beans. Scatter over the chillies
and pimentos and season to taste with salt and pepper. Mix the cheeses together
in a bowl and sprinkle on top.

☀ Bake in the preheated oven for 5–8 minutes, or until the cheese is melted and
bubbling. Serve immediately.

Crunchy Potato Skins

serves 4

4 potatoes, cooked in their skins

2 streaky bacon rashers

115 g/4 oz blue cheese, crumbled

vegetable oil, for deep-frying

to garnish

crème fraîche or soured cream

fresh chives

☀ Preheat the grill to high. Cut the potatoes in half and scoop out the flesh, leaving a lining about 5 mm/¼ inch thick. Place the flesh in a bowl and cover to keep warm.

☀ Cook the bacon under the grill until crisp. Transfer to a plate and cut into small strips. Combine the bacon and the cheese with the potato flesh.

☀ Heat the oil over a high heat in a deep saucepan or wok to 180–190°C/350–375°F or until a cube of bread browns in 30 seconds. Carefully drop the potato skins into the oil and fry for 3–4 minutes, or until crisp and golden. Remove and drain well on kitchen paper.

☀ Arrange the potato skins on a large plate and fill each with a spoonful of the bacon, cheese and potato mixture, piling it high so that it is almost overflowing. Garnish with a teaspoon of crème fraîche and chives and serve immediately.

Hummus and Tapenade

to make the hummus:

☀ Put all the ingredients into a food processor and process to form a fairly smooth paste. Using the pulse button, slowly blend in the hot water to give a dipping consistency. Add salt and pepper to taste.

☀ Spoon into a small serving dish, cover and refrigerate until required. Serve with the vegetable crudités.

to make the tapenade:

☀ Put the olives, capers, garlic, thyme, mustard and anchovies with their oil into a food processor and process until smooth. Using the pulse button, slowly blend in the olive oil until a thick purée is formed. Stir in the brandy or water and add pepper to taste.

☀ Spoon into a small serving dish, cover and store in the refrigerator until required. Serve, scattered with parsley, with the vegetable crudités.

hummus

makes 450 g/1 lb

400 g/14 oz canned chickpeas, drained

2 tbsp tahini

4–6 tbsp virgin olive oil

4–6 tbsp lemon juice

2–3 garlic cloves, crushed

1–2 tbsp hot water

salt and pepper

to serve

red and orange pepper strips, celery sticks and cucumber sticks

tapenade

makes 500 g/1 lb 2 oz

225 g/8 oz stoned black olives

40 g/1½ oz capers, drained and rinsed if salty

2 garlic cloves, crushed

1 tbsp chopped fresh thyme

1 tsp Dijon mustard

55 g/2 oz canned anchovies, rinsed and patted dry

6 tbsp virgin olive oil

1–2 tbsp brandy or hot water

pepper

2 tsp chopped fresh parsley

to serve

red and orange pepper strips, celery sticks and cucumber sticks

Chorizo and Cheese
Quesadillas

serves 4

115 g/4 oz mozzarella cheese, grated

115 g/4 oz Cheddar cheese, grated

225 g/8 oz cooked chorizo sausage
(casing removed) or ham, diced

4 spring onions, finely chopped

2 fresh green chillies, such as poblano,
deseeded and finely chopped

salt and pepper

8 flour tortillas

vegetable oil, for brushing

 Place the cheeses, chorizo, spring onions, chillies and salt and pepper to taste in a bowl and mix together.

 Divide the mixture between 4 flour tortillas, then top with the remaining tortillas.

 Brush a large, non-stick or heavy-based frying pan with oil and heat over a medium heat. Add 1 quesadilla and cook, pressing it down with a fish slice, for 4–5 minutes, or until the underside is crisp and lightly browned. Turn over and cook the other side until the cheese is melting. Remove from the frying pan and keep warm. Cook the remaining quesadillas individually.

 Cut each quesadilla into quarters, arrange on a warmed plate and serve.

Profiteroles

serves 4

choux pastry
200 ml/7 fl oz water
5 tbsp butter, plus extra for greasing
100 g/3½ oz plain flour
3 eggs, beaten

cream filling
300 ml/10 fl oz double cream
3 tbsp caster sugar
1 tsp vanilla essence

chocolate and brandy sauce
125 g/4½ oz plain chocolate,
broken into small pieces
2½ tbsp butter
6 tbsp water
2 tbsp brandy

Preheat the oven to 200°C/400°F/Gas Mark 6. Grease a large baking sheet with butter.

To make the pastry, put the water and butter into a saucepan and bring to the boil. Meanwhile, sift the flour into a bowl. Remove the pan from the heat and beat in the flour until smooth. Cool for 5 minutes. Beat in enough of the eggs to give the mixture a soft, dropping consistency. Transfer to a piping bag fitted with a 1-cm/½-inch plain nozzle. Pipe small balls onto the baking sheet. Bake for 25 minutes. Remove from the oven. Pierce each ball with a skewer to let steam escape.

To make the filling, whip together the cream, sugar and vanilla essence. Cut the pastry balls almost in half, then fill with cream.

To make the sauce, gently melt the chocolate and butter with the water together in a small saucepan, stirring, until smooth. Stir in the brandy. Serve the profiteroles in individual serving dishes or pile into a pyramid on a raised cake stand. Pour over the sauce and serve.

Viennese
Chocolate

serves 6

5 tbsp double cream

2 tbsp icing sugar

few drops vanilla essence

200 g/7 oz plain chocolate,
broken into pieces

1 litre/1¾ pints milk

1 tbsp caster sugar

☀ Whisk the double cream until soft peaks form, then whisk in the icing sugar and vanilla. Set aside.

☀ Put the chocolate in a heatproof bowl with 225 ml/8 fl oz of the milk. Set over a saucepan of gently simmering water until the chocolate melts, stirring occasionally.

☀ Pour the remaining milk into a saucepan, add the caster sugar and heat gently. Add the chocolate and milk mixture as soon as the chocolate has melted and whisk constantly over the heat for 5 minutes until frothy.

☀ Pour into warmed cups, top with the whipped cream mixture and serve immediately.

☀ Sprinkle with grated chocolate, if desired.

Hot Brandy
Chocolate

serves 4

1 litre/1¾ pints milk

115g/4oz plain chocolate, broken into pieces

2 tbsp sugar

5 tbsp brandy

6 tbsp whipped cream

grated nutmeg or cocoa powder

 Pour the milk into a saucepan and bring to the boil, then remove from the heat.

 Add the chocolate and sugar and stir over a low heat until the chocolate has melted.

 Pour into 4 heatproof glasses and then pour the brandy over the back of a spoon onto the top of each one.

 Finish with a swirl of cream and a sprinkling of nutmeg or cocoa.

Dairy Strawberry
Ice Cream

serves 6

225 g/8 oz caster sugar
150 ml/5 fl oz water
900 g/2 lb fresh strawberries,
plus extra to decorate
juice of ½ lemon
juice of ½ orange
300 ml/10 fl oz whipping cream

Put the sugar and water into a heavy-based saucepan and heat gently, stirring, until the sugar has dissolved. Bring to the boil, then, without stirring, boil for 5 minutes to form a syrup. Towards the end of the cooking time, keep an eye on the mixture to ensure that it does not burn. Immediately remove the syrup from the heat and leave to cool for at least 1 hour.

Meanwhile, push the strawberries through a nylon sieve into a bowl to form a purée. When the syrup is cold, add the strawberry purée to it with the lemon juice and orange juice and stir well together. Whip the cream until it holds its shape. Keep in the refrigerator until ready to use.

If using an ice cream machine, fold the strawberry mixture into the whipped cream, then churn in the machine following the manufacturer's instructions. Alternatively, freeze the strawberry mixture in a freezerproof container, uncovered, for 1–2 hours, or until it begins to set around the edges. Turn the mixture into a bowl and stir with a fork or beat in a food processor until smooth. Fold in the whipped cream. Return to the freezer and freeze for a further 2–3 hours, or until firm. Cover the container with a lid for storing. Serve decorated with strawberries.

Mixed Fruit
Pavlova

serves 4

6 egg whites

pinch of cream of tartar

pinch of salt

275 g/9½ oz caster sugar

600 ml/1 pint double cream

1 tsp vanilla essence

2 kiwi fruit, sliced

250 g/9 oz strawberries,
hulled and sliced

3 ripe peaches, sliced

1 ripe mango, sliced

2 tbsp orange-flavoured liqueur,
such as Cointreau

fresh mint leaves, to decorate

☀ Preheat the oven to 110°C/225°F/Gas Mark 4. Line 3 baking sheets with baking paper, then draw a 22-cm/8½-inch circle in the centre of each one.

☀ Beat the egg whites in a large bowl into stiff peaks. Mix in the cream of tartar and salt. Gradually add 200 g/7 oz of the sugar. Beat for 2 minutes until glossy.

☀ Fill a piping bag with the meringue mixture and pipe enough to fill each circle, doming them slightly in the centre. Bake in the oven for 3 hours. Remove from the oven and leave to cool.

☀ Whip the cream, vanilla essence and the remaining sugar together in a bowl. Place the fruit in a separate bowl and stir in the liqueur. Place one meringue circle on a serving plate, then spread over one-third of the sugared cream. Spread over one-third of the fruit, then top with a meringue circle. Spread over another third of cream, then another third of fruit. Top with the last meringue circle.

☀ Spread over the remaining cream, followed by the remaining fruit. Decorate with mint leaves and serve.

Marshmallow
Float

serves 4

225 g/8 oz plain chocolate,
broken into pieces

900 ml/1½ pints milk

3 tbsp caster sugar

8 marshmallows

 Finely chop the chocolate with a knife or in a food processor. Do not over-process or the chocolate will melt.

 Pour the milk into a saucepan and bring to just below boiling point. Remove the saucepan from the heat and whisk in the sugar and the chocolate.

Pour into warmed mugs or heatproof glasses, top with a marshmallow or two and serve immediately.

Top Ten Movies

Throw the duvet on the sofa, grab your favourite moreish treats and snuggle down with your girlie pals. It's time for a movie.

Movies for the female audience are now big business, and listed below are a few of the best. If you haven't seen any of them, here's a run down, and if you can't remember them, here's a reminder...

Jerry McGuire (1996) 138 mins. This film is funny, romantic and upbeat – although it may prompt a tear or two. Sports agent Jerry Maguire (*Tom Cruise*) is sacked and strikes out on his own with only one remaining client, Rod Tidwell (*Cuba Gooding Jr.*), and 26-year-old single mother, Dorothy Boyd (*Renee Zellweger*) to support him in his new venture.

An Officer and a Gentleman (1982) 126 mins. Feeling that his life is lacking direction, loner Zach Mayo (*Richard Gere*) enlists in the Navy. During his 13-week boot camp, he explores discipline, friendship and, ultimately, love. This film was nominated for 7 Oscars and the closing scene has been described as a classic of movie romance.

Dirty Dancing (1987) 96 mins. Set in the mid-60s, Baby (*Jennifer Grey*) is stuck on summer vacation with her parents. To make her holiday more interesting, Baby attends the dancing classes and suddenly her life changes when she meets the instructor, Johnny Castle (*Patrick Swayze*). Johnny teaches Baby the steps to a new dance and Baby soon discovers herself and her love for Johnny.

Pretty Woman (1990) 119 mins. This classic Hollywood fairy tale takes off when corporate big shot Edward Lewis (*Richard Gere*) meets no-nonsense call-girl Vivian Ward (*Julia Roberts*), while in LA for a week. Edward hires Vivian to accompany him to a series of business functions, but both get more than they bargained for!

Love Actually (2003) 128 mins. The film is essentially about love in all shapes and sizes – romantic love, puppy love, platonic love and unrequited love. The main plot centres upon the British Prime Minister (*Hugh Grant*) and his assistant, Natalie (*Martine McCutcheon*).

Bridget Jones (2001) 95 mins. Single, thirty-something Bridget Jones (*Renee Zellweger*) records her brilliantly funny search for Mr. Right. The ditzy and loveable Bridget finds two candidates: the sexy and successful Daniel Cleaver (*Hugh Grant*) and the seemingly rude and haughty Mark Darcy (*Colin Firth*). Which will she choose? Every girl's dream dilemma!

Pride & Prejudice (2005) 127 mins. Based on Jane Austen's classic novel, this film is set in the 18th century and tells the tale of the five Bennet sisters and their search for love. Sit back and enjoy the sparkling chemistry between Elizabeth (*Keira Knightley*) and Mr. Darcy (*Matthew Macfadyen*).

Grease (1978) 110 mins. A great musical, comedy and light romance movie. In the summer of 1958, Danny (*John Travolta*) and Sandy (*Olivia Newton-John*) fall in love. Forced to go their separate ways at the end of summer, they eventually end up in the same high school class. Their reunion, however, is anything but simple.

Romy and Michele's High School Reunion (1997) 91 mins. Romy and Michele (*Mira Sorvino* and *Lisa Kudrow*) have been friends since high school and a decade later the reunion party looms. They plan complete makeovers and new identities and head for the party full of hope. This film is funny, warm and at times cruel, but with a bizarre yet magical ending.

Top Gun (1986) 110 mins. Pilot Pete Mitchell (*Tom Cruise*) is sent to Miramar Naval Air Station for advanced training. Mitchell soon spots and seduces civilian consultant Charlotte Blackwood (*Kelly McGillis*). Tragedy strikes his professional life, but Pete tries to regain his nerve and return to the skies. Classic 80s film with fantastic flight scenes and a great sound-track.

Elegant Suppers

Every girl loves the chance to dress up, and what better

opportunity than an elegant supper with your closest friends?

Think sophistication, chic and that little black dress that rarely gets

an outing. This fabulous chapter will help you plan the perfect

posh supper, complete with champagne cocktails and even

tips on writing an after-dinner speech!

Roasted Asparagus
with Mountain Ham

serves 12

2 tbsp Spanish olive oil

6 slices serrano ham

12 asparagus spears

pepper

to serve

aïoli (see page 17)

☀ Preheat the oven to 200°C/400°F/Gas Mark 6. Put half the olive oil in a roasting tin that will hold the asparagus spears in a single layer and swirl it around so that it covers the base. Cut each slice of serrano ham in half lengthways.

☀ Trim the ends of the asparagus spears, then wrap a slice of ham around the stem end of each spear. Place the wrapped spears in the prepared roasting tin and lightly brush the ham and asparagus with the remaining olive oil. Season the spears with pepper.

☀ Roast the asparagus spears in the oven for about 10 minutes, depending on the thickness of the asparagus, until tender but still firm. Do not overcook the asparagus spears as it is important that they are still firm, so that you can pick them up with your fingers.

☀ Serve the roasted asparagus with mountain ham piping hot, accompanied by a bowl of aïoli for dipping.

Cracked Marinated Olives

serves 8

450 g/1 lb can or jar unstoned
large green olives, drained
4 garlic cloves, peeled
2 tsp coriander seeds
1 small lemon
4 sprigs of fresh thyme
4 feathery stalks of fennel
2 small fresh red chillies (optional)
pepper
Spanish extra virgin olive oil,
to cover

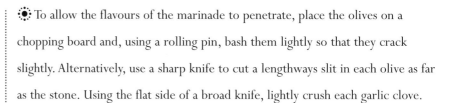

To allow the flavours of the marinade to penetrate, place the olives on a chopping board and, using a rolling pin, bash them lightly so that they crack slightly. Alternatively, use a sharp knife to cut a lengthways slit in each olive as far as the stone. Using the flat side of a broad knife, lightly crush each garlic clove.

Using a pestle and mortar, crack the coriander seeds. Cut the lemon, with its rind, into small chunks.

Put the olives, garlic, coriander seeds, lemon chunks, thyme sprigs, fennel and chillies, if using, in a large bowl and toss together. Season with pepper to taste, but you should not need to add salt as conserved olives are usually salty enough. Pack the ingredients tightly into a glass jar with a lid. Pour in enough olive oil to cover the olives, then seal the jar tightly.

Leave the olives at room temperature for 24 hours, then marinate in the refrigerator for at least 1 week but preferably 2 weeks before serving. From time to time, gently give the jar a shake to re-mix the ingredients. Return the olives to room temperature and remove from the oil to serve. Provide cocktail sticks for spearing the olives.

Mixed Sushi Rolls

serves 4–6

4 sheets nori (seaweed) for rolling

for the rice

250 g/9 oz sushi rice

2 tbsp rice vinegar

1 tsp caster sugar

½ tsp salt

for the fillings

50 g/1¾ oz smoked salmon

4-cm/1½-inch piece cucumber, peeled, deseeded and cut into matchsticks

40 g/1½ oz cooked peeled prawns

1 small avocado, stoned, peeled, thinly sliced and tossed in lemon juice

to serve

wasabi (Japanese horseradish sauce)

tamari (wheat-free soy sauce)

pink pickled ginger

☀ Put the rice into a saucepan and cover with cold water. Bring to the boil, reduce the heat, cover and simmer for 15–20 minutes, or until the rice is tender and the water has been absorbed. Drain and transfer to a bowl. Mix the vinegar, sugar and salt together, then, using a spatula, stir well into the rice. Cover with a damp cloth and leave to cool.

☀ To make the rolls, lay a clean bamboo mat over a chopping board. Lay a sheet of nori, shiny side down, on the mat. Spread a quarter of the rice mixture over the nori, using wet fingers to press it down evenly, leaving a 1-cm/½-in margin at the top and bottom. For smoked salmon and cucumber rolls, lay the salmon over the rice and arrange the cucumber in a line across the centre. For the prawn rolls, lay the prawns and avocado in a line across the centre.

☀ Carefully hold the nearest edge of the mat, then, using the mat as a guide, roll up the nori tightly to make a neat tube of rice enclosing the filling. Seal the uncovered edge with a little water, then roll the sushi off the mat. Repeat to make 3 more rolls. Using a wet knife, cut each roll into 8 pieces and stand upright on a platter. Serve the rolls with wasabi, tamari and pickled ginger.

Roast Beef

serves 8

1 prime rib of beef joint,
weighing 2.7 kg/6 lb
salt and pepper
2 tsp dry English mustard
3 tbsp plain flour
300 ml/10 fl oz red wine
300 ml/10 fl oz beef stock
2 tsp Worcestershire sauce (optional)

to serve

Yorkshire pudding and
vegetables (optional)

☀ Preheat the oven to 230°C/450°F/Gas Mark 8. Season the meat to taste with salt and pepper. Rub in the mustard and 1 tablespoon of the flour. Place the meat in a roasting tin and roast in the oven for 15 minutes. Reduce the temperature to 190°C/ 375°F/Gas Mark 5 and cook for 15 minutes per 450 g/1 lb, plus 15 minutes (1¾ hours for this joint) for rare beef or 20 minutes per 450 g/1 lb, plus 20 minutes (2 hours 20 minutes) for medium beef. Baste the meat from time to time to keep it moist. Remove the meat from the oven and place on a warmed serving plate, cover with foil and leave in a warm place for 10–15 minutes.

☀ To make the gravy, pour off most of the fat from the tin, leaving behind the meat juices. Place the tin on the hob over a medium heat and stir the juices and any sediment. Sprinkle in the remaining flour and quickly mix into the juices with a small whisk. When you have a smooth paste, gradually add the wine and most of the stock, whisking constantly. Bring to the boil, reduce the heat to a gentle simmer and cook for 2–3 minutes. Season to taste with salt and pepper and add the remaining stock, if needed, and a little Worcestershire sauce, if you like.

☀ Carve the meat into slices and serve on warmed plates with Yorkshire pudding and vegetables, if liked.

Roasted Root Vegetables

serves 4-6

3 parsnips, cut into 5-cm/2-in chunks

4 baby turnips, quartered

3 carrots, cut into 5-cm/2-in chunks

450 g/1 lb butternut squash, peeled and cut into 5-cm/2-in chunks

450 g/1 lb sweet potatoes, peeled and cut into 5-cm/2-in chunks

2 garlic cloves, finely chopped

2 tbsp chopped fresh rosemary

2 tbsp chopped fresh thyme

2 tsp chopped fresh sage

3 tbsp olive oil

salt and pepper

to garnish

2 tbsp chopped fresh mixed herbs, such as parsley, thyme and mint

☀ Preheat the oven to 220°C/425°F/Gas Mark 7.

☀ Arrange all the vegetables in a single layer in a large roasting tin. Scatter over the garlic and the herbs. Pour over the oil and season well with salt and pepper.

☀ Toss all the ingredients together until they are well mixed and coated with the oil (you can leave the vegetables to marinate at this stage to allow the flavours to be absorbed).

☀ Roast the vegetables at the top of the oven for 50–60 minutes until they are cooked and nicely browned. Turn the vegetables over halfway through the cooking time.

☀ Serve with a good handful of fresh herbs scattered on top and a final sprinkling of salt and pepper to taste.

Pan-fried
Lamb Noisettes

serves 4

1 large aubergine, cut into 16 slices

3 tbsp olive oil

salt and pepper

3 large garlic cloves, crushed

1 fresh red jalapeño chilli, deseeded
and finely chopped

8 lamb noisettes

fresh coriander sprigs, to garnish

for the pesto

115 g/4 oz shelled fresh, frozen or
canned broad beans

salt and pepper

1 large garlic clove, crushed

1 tbsp chopped fresh coriander

100 ml/3½ fl oz extra virgin olive oil

1½ tbsp freshly grated Parmesan
cheese

First make the pesto. If using fresh or frozen broad beans, cook in lightly salted boiling water for 10 minutes, or until tender. Drain and put into a food processor with the garlic and coriander. Using the pulse button, finely chop. With the motor running, slowly pour in the extra virgin olive oil. When all the oil has been incorporated, scrape the pesto into a bowl and add salt and pepper to taste and the Parmesan cheese. Spoon into a serving bowl, cover and refrigerate until required.

Meanwhile, arrange the aubergine slices on a large baking tray and sprinkle with olive oil, reserving 1 teaspoon, then scatter over the garlic and chilli. Leave for at least 30 minutes. Preheat the grill to medium and cover the grill rack with foil. Arrange a single layer of aubergine slices on the grill rack and cook under the preheated grill for 3–5 minutes, turning once, until tender and beginning to crisp. Remove and keep warm while cooking the remaining slices and the lamb.

Meanwhile, preheat a non-stick frying pan over a medium heat. Season the lamb noisettes, add to the pan and brown on all sides, then cook for 6–8 minutes on each side. Arrange 4 aubergine slices on each serving plate, top with the lamb and serve, garnished with coriander sprigs, with a spoonful of pesto.

Cannelloni with
Ham and Ricotta

serves 4

2 tbsp olive oil

2 onions, chopped

2 garlic cloves, finely chopped

1 tbsp shredded fresh basil

800 g/1 lb 12 oz chopped tomatoes

1 tbsp tomato purée

salt and pepper

350 g/12 oz dried cannelloni tubes

butter, for greasing

100 g/4 oz ricotta cheese

115 g/4 oz cooked ham, diced

1 egg

50 g/2 oz freshly grated pecorino
cheese

☀ Preheat the oven to 180°C/350°F/Gas Mark 4. Heat the olive oil in a large, heavy-based frying pan. Add the onions and garlic and cook over a low heat, stirring occasionally, for 5 minutes, or until the onion is softened. Add the basil, chopped tomatoes with their juices and tomato purée, and season to taste with salt and pepper. Reduce the heat and simmer for 30 minutes, or until thickened.

☀ Meanwhile, bring a large, heavy-based saucepan of lightly salted water to the boil. Add the dried cannelloni tubes, return to the boil, and cook for 8–10 minutes, or until tender but still firm to the bite. Using a slotted spoon, transfer the cannelloni tubes to a large plate and pat dry with kitchen paper.

☀ Grease a large, shallow ovenproof dish with butter. Mix the ricotta, ham and egg together in a bowl and season to taste with salt and pepper. Using a teaspoon, fill the cannelloni tubes with the ricotta, ham and egg mixture and place in a single layer in the dish. Pour the tomato sauce over the cannelloni and sprinkle with the grated pecorino cheese. Bake in the preheated oven for 30 minutes, or until golden brown. Serve immediately.

Roasted Salmon with
Lemon and Herbs

serves 4

6 tbsp extra virgin olive oil

1 onion, sliced

1 leek, sliced

juice of ½ lemon

2 tbsp chopped fresh parsley

2 tbsp chopped fresh dill

500 g/1 lb 2 oz salmon fillets

salt and pepper

freshly cooked baby spinach
leaves, to serve

to garnish

lemon slices

fresh dill sprigs

☀ Preheat the oven to 200°C/400°F/Gas Mark 6.

☀ Heat 1 tablespoon of the oil in a frying pan over a medium heat. Add the onion and leek and cook, stirring, for 4 minutes, or until slightly softened.

☀ Meanwhile, place the remaining oil in a small bowl with the lemon juice and herbs and season to taste with salt and pepper. Stir together well. Rinse the fish under cold running water, then pat dry with kitchen paper. Arrange the fish in a shallow ovenproof baking dish.

☀ Remove the frying pan from the heat and spread the onion and leek over the fish. Pour the oil mixture over the top, ensuring that everything is well coated.

☀ Roast in the centre of the oven for 10 minutes, or until the fish is cooked through.

☀ Arrange the cooked spinach on serving plates. Remove the fish and vegetables from the oven and arrange on top of the spinach. Garnish with lemon slices and dill sprigs and serve immediately.

Easy Orange Cheesecake

serves 6

115 g/4 oz digestive biscuits

55 g/2 oz butter, plus extra for greasing

225 g/8 oz curd cheese

150 ml/5 fl oz natural yogurt

½ packet orange jelly (100–115 g/ 3½–4 oz), torn into cubes

1 tbsp sugar

grated rind and juice of 1 orange

200 g/7 oz canned mandarin orange segments, drained

☀ Break up the biscuits and process in batches in a blender to make crumbs. Melt the butter in a small saucepan over a low heat. Remove the pan from the heat and stir in the biscuit crumbs. Lightly grease a 20-cm/8-in loose-based flan tin, then press the buttery crumbs into it. Place in the refrigerator to chill until the crust has set.

☀ Meanwhile, clean the blender, place the curd cheese and yogurt in the clean blender and process to combine.

☀ Heat 3–4 tablespoons water in a small saucepan, then remove from the heat and add the jelly. Stir until dissolved, then stir in the sugar and the orange rind and juice. Add the mixture to the blender and process until smooth. Pour the filling into the biscuit crumb case and chill in the refrigerator for 2 hours, or until set.

☀ Carefully remove the cheesecake from the tin and place on a serving plate. Arrange the mandarin segments around the edge of the cheesecake and serve.

Kiwi Sorbet

serves 6

700 g/1 lb 9 oz kiwi fruit
4 tbsp orange juice
140 g/5 oz caster sugar
strip of thinly pared lemon rind

☀ To peel a kiwi, cut a thin slice off both ends, then stand it upright on a chopping board and slice off the remainder of the skin vertically in strips. Try not to remove too much of the flesh. Peel all the kiwis and cut into quarters. Place them in the blender with the orange juice and process to a purée.

☀ Put the sugar and lemon rind in a heavy-based saucepan and pour in 175 ml/6 fl oz water. Bring to the boil, stirring until the sugar has dissolved, then remove the pan from the heat and set aside to cool.

☀ Remove and discard the lemon rind from the sugar syrup. Stir in the kiwi fruit purée and mix well. Pour the mixture into a freezer-proof container, cover and place in the freezer for 1 hour until ice crystals have formed around the edges. Scoop the sorbet into the blender and process until smooth. Return to the container and replace the container in the freezer for 1 hour.

☀ Process the sorbet in the blender again, then return to the freezer. Repeat this process once more, then freeze until firm. Transfer the container to the refrigerator 10 minutes before serving to allow the sorbet to soften slightly.

Raspberry Creams

serves 4

450 g/1 lb fresh raspberries
175 g/6 oz low-fat cottage cheese
3 tbsp sugar
150 ml/5 fl oz low-fat natural yogurt
icing sugar, to decorate

☀ Reserving a few whole raspberries to decorate, use the back of a spoon to push the raspberries and cottage cheese through a nylon sieve into a bowl.

☀ Stir the sugar and yogurt into the raspberry mixture and stir to blend, then spoon into individual serving dishes. Cover and refrigerate for about 1 hour.

☀ Serve chilled, decorated with the reserved raspberries and dusted with sifted icing sugar.

Bellini

 Pour boiling water over the peaches to scald them. Drain, then peel and chop them, discarding the stones.

Put the chopped peaches into a food processor and process until smooth.

Divide the peach mixture between 2 champagne flutes. Stir in the champagne or sparkling wine, mixing with a swizzle stick.

Serve at once with a few amaretti biscuits.

Champagne Cocktail

serves 1

1 sugar cube
2 dashes Angostura bitters
1 measure brandy
champagne, chilled

The classic champagne cocktail can be too sweet for some. It is the brandy that gives the treat and the kick, so you could leave out the sugar!

* Place the sugar cube with the drops of bitters in the base of a chilled flute.

* Pour on the brandy and top up slowly with champagne.

Iced Coffee and Peppermint Slush

serves 2

400 ml/14 fl oz milk

200 ml/7 fl oz coffee syrup

100 ml/3½ fl oz peppermint syrup

1 tbsp chopped fresh mint leaves

4 ice cubes

to decorate

grated chocolate

sprigs of fresh mint

☀ Pour the milk, coffee syrup and peppermint syrup into a food processor and process gently until combined.

☀ Add the mint and ice cubes and process until a slushy consistency has been achieved.

☀ Pour the mixture into glasses. Scatter over the grated chocolate, decorate with sprigs of fresh mint and serve.

Writing an After-Dinner Speech

❋ It's been a very special night in with the girls, and you've hosted an elegant supper that everyone will remember. Maybe you've been celebrating a special occasion in your life, or that of one of your girlfriends. It's your birthday, or someone's starting a new job, getting married or, sadly, moving away from the area. What better way to end a formal dinner than with an appropriate after-dinner speech that captures the spirit of the evening?

❋ Think carefully about the person or event that your speech is going to be about. Think about what you know about that person. Jot down notes of facts, memories, stories or anything that you associate with them. Start thinking well in advance, so there's no pressure on you. You'll find that once the ideas start to come, the rest will start to flow naturally.

❋ If you are going to use humour in a speech you might as well start as you mean to go on, so begin on a light-hearted note and raise a laugh. Nothing will get your friends on board faster than a bit of wit, and then you can move on to the meat of your speech.

❋ Of course, what you are going to say will vary enormously depending on what you are celebrating, but there are certain rules and guidelines that will stand you in good stead on practically any occasion. First and foremost, know your audience. Of course, they are good friends, so you can take a few liberties, but some may be more easily offended than others. Make the first part of your speech a word of welcome and a reminder of why you are all together. Also try to strike a tone that suits the occasion – clearly, a speech delivered at a birthday dinner or a hen party should have a different tone from one at which you are saying goodbye to someone.

❈ ❈ ❈

❀ The middle is the part of a speech where there is the greatest scope for the use of humour. This is the place for shaggy dog stories, one-liners or pearls of witty wisdom. Take the opportunity to remind everyone of the good times, the funny moments, the embarrassing behaviour that you'd all rather forget but can't help laughing about. Make sure that your reminiscences involve everyone – some people may feel excluded if you refer to memorable times that they didn't share. The one rule about humour in a speech is: keep it relevant. It must arise naturally from the subject or be used to illustrate a point, otherwise it just sounds forced.

❀ The last part of your speech should look forward to the future, whether that is the happiness of your best mate who is marrying or the hope of seeing your departing girlfriend at another party soon. There is only one thing to remember about composing the ending to a speech: it must obviously be an ending. There is nothing worse than coming to the end of your speech only to find that your audience doesn't realize it's finished! Perhaps the surest way to close your speech is by proposing a toast. Thank everyone for being there, make sure their glasses are charged, and drink to the particular friend, or just to yourselves and the promise of getting together again for another Elegant Supper.

Index